A BOBBY'S JOB

IMAGES OF
POLICING IN CHESHIRE

MUSEUM OF POLICING IN CHESHIRE

COMPILED BY WILL BROWN

The
History
Press

This book is dedicated to
all former and current members
of the Cheshire Constabulary.

First published 2014

The History Press
The Mill, Brimscombe Port
Stroud, Gloucestershire, GL5 2QG
www.thehistorypress.co.uk

© Museum of Policing in Cheshire, 2014

The right of Museum of Policing in Cheshire to be identified as the
Authors of this work has been asserted in accordance with the
Copyright, Designs and Patents Act 1988.

British Library Cataloguing in Publication Data.
A catalogue record for this book is available from the British Library.

ISBN 978 0 7509 5220 0

Typesetting and origination by The History Press
Printed and bound in Great Britain by
Marston Book Services Ltd, Oxfordshire

CONTENTS

FOREWORD

This book is a fascinating read for anyone who wants an insight into the lives of the ordinary men and women who chose to spend their working lives keeping the public of Cheshire safe. It starts with 'Old Jack Sutton' prior to 1857 and tells many wonderful stories of straw helmets, horse allowances, women officers being refused parity of pay and a Chief Constable's labrador. It shows how officers were equipped to deal with diverse challenges, from escorting elephants to quelling riots, from horse allowances to the first Sunbeam police car to Vauxhall Vivas. There is much that seems alien to modern-day officers and many of the buildings in this book no longer exist or have been put to other uses. However, amongst the faces looking out of these black and white photographs and through the stories so carefully researched for this book, we can see a little of the personalities and commitment that maintained law and order in the county then and that also built the foundations of modern-day policing and the Cheshire Constabulary as it is now. Values of courage, resilience, service and compassion were always required in British policing and that is still true today.

The Cheshire Constabulary is a highly respected force and one that I am immensely proud to have been a member of since I joined it as a young police constable in 1986. I am conscious in my years of policing that we rely upon the work of those who went before us as we continuously strive to improve in all we do. As Isaac Newton put it, we are 'standing on the shoulders of giants'. Some of those giants feature in this book, others put their efforts into creating the Museum of Policing in Cheshire, which I recommend to you as an enthralling place for all ages to visit. The Force is indebted to those individuals who voluntarily give their time to preserve and share our history.

This book gives you a taste of the treasures held by the museum and we are grateful to Will Brown (supported by Jim Talbot) for the diligent work he has put into creating it. As a young officer, I remember Will as a very professional senior detective and I now see those skills in investigation manifest in the stories he has discovered that bring these pictures to life.

I hope you enjoy this book as much I have and that it prompts you to reflect on the demands on officers past and present who serve the public doing 'a bobby's job'.

Helen King QPM MA(Oxon) MA, Deputy Chief Constable of Cheshire, 2014

ACKNOWLEDGEMENTS

I am grateful to the committee of the Museum of Policing in Cheshire, chaired by Deputy Chief Constable Helen King, for the enthusiastic support they have given to this project and, in particular, I would like to thank Jim Talbot, a trustee of the museum, for his help with the research involved. Jim has worked tirelessly for a number of years researching original force records, and has amassed a formidable database of over 14,000 names and details of officers who have served not only in the Cheshire Constabulary, but also in the other forces, which at one time or another have merged into the force. Jim regularly responds to requests from the descendants of former officers, not only in the UK but worldwide, who are researching their family history.

Whilst the majority of images reproduced are taken from the museum collection, I would like to give a special thanks to the following individuals for their kindness in allowing personally held family photographs to be used in this publication: John P. Birchall, Mark Samuals, Christine Davies, Francis Bradley, Anthony Jones, Heather Jones, Peter Barton, Keith Foster, Maurice Titmuss, Michael Hunt, Clive Haycocks, Nick Latham, Alan Spann, Bill Graham, Gerry Mort, Gwilym and Carmen Williams, Bill Havers and Mike Smyth. Thanks also to the many retired officers and the relatives of former officers – too many to mention here individually – who have previously donated photographs to the museum, some of which have been reproduced in this book. I am grateful to the many former colleagues that I approached in order to tap their particular knowledge in respect of aspects of my research, and, finally, thanks must go to the staff at the Cheshire Archives and Local Studies in Chester, and the staff at the Constabulary Headquarters at Winsford, for their help and assistance.

Taken in around the 1850s, here we see a constable of the Warrington Borough force photographed whilst patrolling his beat in Bridge Street. At the time there were only nine constables to police a population of 24,000. By 1864, the number of constables had risen to twenty-three. The uniform the officer is wearing was adopted in 1847 when the force was formed. Helmets were introduced towards the end of the 1860s. (Courtesy of Warrington Museum & Art Gallery)

INTRODUCTION

The local government boundary changes in 1974 changed the shape of the county of Cheshire, which had remained the same for several hundreds of years; areas in the north-east of the county, places such as Stalybridge, Hyde, Stockport and Altrincham, became part of Greater Manchester and the north Wirral area, Birkenhead, Wallasey and surrounding smaller towns, became part of Merseyside. The new Cheshire now included Warrington and Widnes, which had previously been within Lancashire. This book charts the story of policing in Cheshire through images taken from the extensive photographic archive held by the museum, as well as images provided by private individuals, and covers the period from the early part of the nineteenth century when police forces were formed through to the 1970s. Whilst focusing mainly on the pre-1974 county, including the forces that had been previously amalgamated, it also embraces images of policing in the former Lancashire area now part of Cheshire.

The Cheshire Constabulary came into being on 20 April 1857, when the force was established following the County and Borough Police Act of 1856, which obliged the justices to establish a paid police force for each county. Some counties such as Lancashire had already formed forces following the County Police Act of 1839. The initial establishment of the force was comprised of one chief constable, nine superintendents, two inspectors, fifteen sergeants and 143 constables. The force was divided into nine divisions, which roughly followed the same districts as had been established under the old hundred system. The starting pay of a constable was 18/-d per week, which today would have a spending worth of less than £40.

In 1857 there were already a number of smaller forces in existence within the county area: the city of Chester and the boroughs of Congleton, Macclesfield and Stockport had established their own forces in 1836 following the Municipal Corporations Act of 1835, which permitted towns with a population of more than 5,000 inhabitants to maintain its own police force, and these were administered by watch committees made up of magistrates and local councillors. Birkenhead and Stalybridge also established their own forces, which were administered by boards of commissioners comprising of local people. Warrington also established its own force in 1847.

Sir Robert Peel, on forming the Metropolitan Police in 1829, seemed keen to ensure that the new police were not perceived as a military force. In previous times, the military had often been called upon to quell instances of public disorder, most notably in Manchester in 1819 when eleven people were killed and several hundred injured in a charge by untrained yeomanry in what became known as the Peterloo Massacre. The military ethos was, however, often reflected in early policing by the appointment of former military officers as chief constables and also many of the recruits who were former soldiers. The early uniform of blue, however, did not follow military style and the stovepipe top hat was in part intended to convey to the public an image of a civilian in uniform. The introduction of helmets from the 1860s onwards, and in Cheshire particularly the shako hat, marked a departure as both were clearly styled on military headgear of the era.

The first issue of uniform to the Cheshire force included, for sergeants and constables: two frock coats, two pairs of trousers one hat and one stock. The stock was a piece of leather likened to a collar about 4in wide and worn around the neck beneath the tunic, the purpose of this piece of equipment was to give protection against 'garrotting', which was quite a common form of criminal assault in those times. There is evidence that the stock still formed part of police uniform as late as 1883, when records relate the disciplining of a Warrington constable for failing to wear his stock; the officer was fined 1/-d.

It would seem that at first the new chief constable had a motley collection of men to mould into a disciplined force and records from the time suggest that discipline was rigorously enforced, as shown by the many instances of dismissal that resulted in a high turnover of personnel. Training was very much 'on the job', with organised training coming much later towards the end of the nineteenth century. Drunkenness on duty appears to have been a particular problem and a frequent reason for dismissal. Study of the conduct register of this period proves at least one thing: if the policeman had little 'brain', he at least had 'brawn' and courage. A great majority of the discipline charges indicated the tendency when drunk for some officers to take on 'all comers', as in the case of Constable James Bloyand in 1862, who is recorded as being drunk on duty and engaging in a wrestling bout in a field in the presence of forty or fifty persons; following which he was dismissed.

The harsh conditions endured by officers in the early days is shown in the official order book of the Hyde Division for 1858, which contains an order for a sergeant and nine constables to march overnight to Chester, some 40 miles on indifferent roads, to perform duty the following day at the Royal Agricultural Society's show. It would seem that despite the already extensive railway network available as a mode of transport, that this was frowned upon. The fitness of the officers to perform their duties on arrival at Chester the following morning is clearly questionable.

Another hardship faced by officers was the restrictions placed on their private lives and these were quite draconian. Some of these restrictions, albeit somewhat modified, continued well into the twentieth century. With poor pay and conditions, which included only one rest day a month, it is no wonder that many left the force voluntarily after only a short period of service. Even in their off-duty time, officers were not allowed to leave their place of duty without the written permission of the superintendent and this would often only be granted in extreme circumstances. The vetting of men applying to join the force was often scant, and there are several cases recorded of men who were later found to be undesirable becoming members of the force, as well as several examples of army deserters being engaged who were later discovered and dismissed.

The case of Edward Hindley, who joined the Cheshire force in 1874, is perhaps a good illustration. The records show him to be 19 years of age on appointment – the minimum age he could join the force. He was posted to Bollington, near Macclesfield and whilst stationed there he met and married a 27-year-old local woman, and they started a family. In 1876, with two years' service, Edward absconded from his place of duty, which was then an offence, and he was later apprehended and taken before the magistrates at Macclesfield where he was fined £2 with costs or two months' imprisonment. The case reported in the *Macclesfield Courier* alludes to him also being a deserter from the Royal Artillery; it also emerged that at the time of his appointment he had only been 16 years of age. Following his problems with the police and military authorities, he returned to his former trade of shoemaker in the family business at Barnton, near Northwich. He later rose to prominence in the area as a rich and successful business entrepreneur, owning land and property including the Weaver Refining Co. Ltd at Acton Bridge. Hindley also became a Cheshire county councillor and Justice of the Peace. He died in 1935, leaving a large estate.

Men in the county force were frequently transferred between divisions, which was clearly disruptive, particularly to those with families, and very often these postings would only be for a matter of months, before they were on the move again. Records show that most officers were transferred on numerous occasions during their service. Men joining borough and city forces obviously remained in that area throughout their service. The main reason for the continual upheaval of county officers appears to have been a perception amongst the hierarchy that if they were left in a particular area for too long they may become too familiar with the local inhabitants, which in turn may lead to allegations of favouritism towards particular groups or individuals. In 1897, sixty-four residents, mainly tradespeople, from the village of Hazel Grove near Stockport sent a signed a petition to the chief constable of Cheshire requesting the removal of a particular sergeant, claiming that he performed his duties 'in a malicious, domineering, meddlesome and objectionable manner'. The chief constable apparently found no grounds to justify his removal and the officer remained where he was. Whether the sergeant performed his duties with too much zeal, or whether the locals resented his impartiality in maintaining law and order, is not known.

Mention has been made of the family life of officers in those early days. In the case of the rural policeman, his wife played an important role in supporting her husband, often having to deal with persons calling at their cottage to report matters when the officer was absent. It is worth mentioning here that rural beat officers' wives freely continued with this type of assistance until the role of resident rural beat officer ceased not that many years ago. In the early days, policemen's wives also rendered assistance as police matrons to look after the welfare and needs of females who were detained in custody.

As policing progressed into the twentieth century, conditions for rank and file officers improved with the Weekly Rest Day Act of 1910, and the creation of the Police Federation in 1919. The superintendents' horse and gig eventually gave way to motor transport and the development of motor patrols in the 1920s and '30s to meet the increase in road traffic. Training improved, culminating in the district training centres being opened after the Second World War. The challenges of policing during the wartime years, when many regular officers were serving in the armed forces, were supported by the recruitment of significant numbers of special constables and the recall of some retired officers. In 1946, the first policewomen were appointed to the force and, in 1947, the former borough forces of Stalybridge, Hyde, Macclesfield and Congleton were amalgamated with the Cheshire Constabulary. This was followed, in 1949, by the merger of the Chester City force and later, in 1967, the amalgamation of the Stockport, Wallasey and Birkenhead forces. Between 1967 and 1974, the strength of the Cheshire Constabulary was in excess of 3,000, making it one of the largest provincial forces at that time.

The police service in Cheshire has a proud tradition, and it is hoped that the images contained in this book exemplify that pride, which forms a cornerstone of policing.

Anyone wishing to learn more about the Museum of Policing in Cheshire can go to the website: www.museumofpolicingincheshire.org.uk. The museum is an independent registered charity and is staffed entirely by volunteers. It is located at Warrington Police Station, Arpley Street, Warrington WA1 1LQ. Groups and individuals are welcome to visit the museum, however, all visits are by appointment only, so to arrange a visit please contact the museum on: 01606 365803.

Will Brown, 2014
(Former Detective Superintendent with the Cheshire Constabulary)

THE VICTORIAN POLICEMAN

Pictured is 'Old Jack Sutton' who was employed as night watchman by Nantwich Town Council prior to the creation of the police force. His presence on the streets at night would have provided some degree of protection for the citizens. He continued in this role beyond the establishment of the force in 1857. Note the seemingly weather-resistant clothing and bullseye lantern slung from his neck. (Cheshire Archives and Local Studies)

A specimen uniform worn by the Macclesfield Borough force upon formation in 1836. Initially, the force consisted of a chief constable and six officers. In this illustration, the officer is seen with a leather holster attached to his belt in which he carried his truncheon. He is also in possession of a lantern. The reason for white trousers is unknown, but may have been adopted to make him more visible. (*History of Macclesfield Borough Police* by C.C. Symonds, 1947)

Captain Thomas Johnnes Smith of the Bedfordshire Militia was appointed chief constable of the new Cheshire Constabulary at a meeting of the full police committee, held at the Crewe Arms Hotel on 3 February 1857. The force became live on 20 April of that year. Captain Smith served until his death in 1877. A contemporary obituary notice ended with the words 'in manner he was distinctively a gentleman'. (Cheshire Constabulary)

Upon inauguration of the force in 1857, Captain Smith established his headquarters at No. 4 Seller Street, Chester – a privately owned house, which is pictured here in the 1960s and has since been demolished. In 1862, the headquarters moved to No. 1 Egerton Street, where it remained until 1870 when premises at No. 113 Foregate Street became the force headquarters. (Museum collection)

John Hindley (pictured) was one of the first recruits to join the force. This photograph depicts the uniform that was adopted, in particular the style of cap with the Prince of Wales' feathers badge. Most forces were still wearing the stovepipe-style top hat. He is holding a pair of Hiatt Darby pattern handcuffs, which were still issued until the late 1960s. John retired as chief superintendent of the North Wirral Division in 1899. (John P. Birchall)

George Edward Oldmeadow joined the Cheshire Constabulary on inauguration. He had previously served with Captain Smith as his clerk in the Bedfordshire Militia. He became the chief clerk at headquarters and his ability as an administrator appears to have been key to the efficient organisation of the early force. In 1858, he was promoted to superintendent and continued as chief clerk until his death in service in 1889. (Mark Samuels)

This early photograph (above) of a group of Cheshire officers, taken in 1878, shows them wearing a cap that has a flat jutting peak similar to a Kepi, and not the original style of cap adopted in 1857 as worn by Constable John Hindley. About this time, helmets were also introduced, although only worn on special occasions when a force order directed. (Museum collection)

The Macclesfield Borough Police, pictured (left) in 1874, when James Etchells (seated centre) was the chief constable. It is interesting that the officers are still wearing the stovepipe hat when by this time most other forces had adopted the helmet, which had first been introduced in 1863 by the Metropolitan Police. (*History of Macclesfield Borough Police* by C.C. Symonds, 1947)

Members of Birkenhead combined police and fire force with early fire tender (*c.* 1880). Many borough and city forces were required to provide a fire-fighting response, and this responsibility only ceased in some forces with the formation of the National Fire Service during the Second World War. It will be noted that the helmets worn by the two supervising officers have no badges; it was not uncommon in those days in some forces for constables only to have a helmet displaying the force badge. (*Maintaining the Queen's Peace*, 1958)

John Bradbury joined the Cheshire Constabulary in 1886. In this photograph, he is holding his shako, which by this time was the day-to-day headdress of the force, although helmets continued to be worn on special occasions. He was stationed at Hyde when this photograph was taken early in his career, and he was one of only eight constables in the force to be awarded the 1911 King George V Coronation Medal. (Christine Davies)

The group of officers pictured (*c.* 1885) are seen wearing spikes on their helmets. Spikes were interchangeable with a ball top and were only worn when specific orders included an item 'with spikes' or 'without spikes'. The two officers wearing medals both have the Khedive's Star awarded for military service in Egypt. Note the leather gaiters being worn by the officers. (Museum collection)

Macclesfield Division officers pictured wearing a lightweight summer tunic (*c.* 1888). At the time, the cost of a constable's greatcoat, tunic and two pairs of trousers amounted to £3 14*s* 4*d*. The lady in the photograph is unknown, but could be the wife of the inspector who is sitting to her right. (Museum collection)

The fourth headquarters of the force was built at No. 142 Foregate Street, Chester, for less than £2,000 and opened in 1886. With added extensions and comprising the two buildings nearest the camera, it served as the force headquarters until 1967 when the new building on Nuns Road became operational. (Cheshire Constabulary)

Congleton Borough Police photographed in 1890 (above, left). The force was established in 1836, with a strength of one superintendent and four constables. In 1889, following a government inspection, the force was declared to be inefficient for want of sufficient strength, which still remained at five. The watch committee was obliged to immediately double the strength and for the first time the force was put into uniform. (Museum collection)

The original Warrington Police Station or 'Bridewell' in Irlam Street (*c.* 1890). This building, which only contained four cells, became inadequate to meet the needs of the expanding town and closed when the present station at Arpley Street was opened in 1901. This building is no longer there. (Museum collection)

A group of officers who have just received a batch of new bicycles (*c.* 1890). It is interesting to note that the superintendent (centre) is holding the only one that appears to be fitted with a lamp! Force orders stipulated that 'a bicycle was also to be kept at headquarters for the purpose of training recruits in the use of same'. (Museum collection)

Nantwich Division officers pictured around 1890 at the rear of Nantwich Police Station in Welsh Row. The officer in the rear row, third from the right, is Constable Alfred Kerns, who tragically died in April 1900 following an incident whilst on duty outside the Hawk Inn at Haslington. He sustained a fractured skull after falling during a scuffle with two men. Both men were charged with manslaughter but were later acquitted. (Museum collection)

The Winsford Waterman's strike of 1892 developed into such serious disorder that the Cheshire Police contingent of 250 officers had to be reinforced by officers from the Lancashire Constabulary and a contingent of Military Hussars, who were billeted locally for the duration of the strike. Several police officers were injured during the ensuing disorder. Officers here are pictured outside the Salt Union offices at Winsford. (Museum collection)

This is a studio photograph of four Cheshire officers taken in 1899, when they were stationed at West Kirkby. Sergeant James Piercy is pictured with constables Thomas Woodward (seated), Albert Sudlow (standing, left) and Thomas Rogers (standing, right). They are wearing helmets as opposed to the normal shako and carrying white-cotton gloves suggesting they may have just performed some special duty. (Museum collection)

The Great Coal Strike of 1893 saw officers from Cheshire drafted to the South Yorkshire coalfields. The Cheshire officers pictured are at Barrow Colliery in Barnsley and are equipped with swords, which were only issued under stringent orders that confined their use to defending life, use in serious riots or against deadly weapons. It is not known whether or not swords were drawn by Cheshire officers during the strike. (Museum collection)

Frodsham Section pictured outside the police station on the High Street (*c.* 1900). The station was built around 1880, to replace Frodshams first police station in Red Lane. The building above closed in the 1970s, when the present station at Ship Street was opened, and is now commercial premises. (Museum collection)

A portrait of Superintendent James Bowyer captured around 1900 when in command of the South Wirral Division based at Abbey Street, Birkenhead. The ornate style of his frock coat and cap is shown to good effect. The North and South Wirral divisions were later merged to become the Wirral Division upon the formation of the Wallasey Borough force in 1913 and the divisional headquarters was then established at Heswall. (Museum collection)

Sergeant Edward Hatton pictured with his section, in around 1899, outside the old Hoylake Police Station in Prussia Road. Hatton joined the force in 1891 after service in the Grenadier Guards. The officers are wearing the lighter weight summer tunics with breast pockets worn without the standard leather belt. PC Saunders (far right) transferred to the newly created Hyde Borough force shortly after the photograph was taken. (Anthony Jones)

The hand ambulance or body cart was kept at police stations and used principally for conveying corpses to local mortuaries. It was also used for taking corpses from the workhouse to a pauper's funeral; apparently, on this macabre journey young children would often run alongside the cortège shouting 'rattle his bones over the stones, he's only an old pauper that nobody owns'. This body cart was used at Dukinfield in the Victorian era. (Museum collection)

Members of the Stalybridge Borough force pictured with the Chief Constable William Chadwick (far left, in a top hat). The photograph is believed to have been taken around 1899 at the time of his retirement, having served as chief constable for thirty-seven years. Prior to his appointment at Stalybridge, he had served as an inspector in the Ashton-under-Lyne force and earlier as a petty constable in the Dukinfield district. (Reproduced courtesy of Tameside Local Studies and Archives)

A portrait of PC Samuel Johnson of the Stockport Borough force taken about 1901. Johnson was a local man who had joined the force in 1891, having previously worked as a warehouseman. The ornate style of helmet worn by the Stockport force at that time is well illustrated in this photograph. (Museum collection)

A group of Stockport Borough officers pictured outside Warren Street Police Station (*c.* 1900). The officer seated on the left is wearing an attachment to his leather belt used to secure a bullseye oil lantern, which was issued for night duty. (Museum collection)

Sergeant William Warburton pictured in the late 1890s. The photograph is believed to have been taken at Hoole Police Station, where recruits received their basic training. Those in civilian clothes are thought to be recruits in training. In June 1900, he saved a man from drowning in the canal at Chester, for which he received an Honorary Testimonial on Parchment from the Royal Humane Society. He retired in 1901. (Courtesy of Heather Jones)

2

EARLY TWENTIETH-CENTURY POLICING

Albert Foster joined the force in 1889. In February 1902, when a sergeant at Northenden, which was then in Cheshire, he, together with another officer PC Lawson, confronted a man named Cotterill who had shot his employer. Cotterill was in possession of two revolvers and fired several shots at the officers, who called on local residents for weapons, and two shotguns were provided. Several further shots were exchanged and Cotterill was fatally wounded by the officers. At the inquest into Cotterill's death, the coroner returned a verdict of justifiable homicide and commended their actions in difficult and dangerous circumstances. Foster retired an inspector in 1921. (Francis May Bradley)

Sergeant Benfield of the Northwich Division pictured in 1902, accompanied by uniform and plain-clothes officers outside the police post in Delamere Forest, where they were engaged on security duties at a temporary military camp. The reason for the troops' presence in the area is unknown, though it is possible it was for an exercise. The police contingent were later complimented by the major-general commanding for their efficiency. (Tony Taylor)

Officers photographed in 1904 outside Broxton Police Station, which was also the headquarters for the Broxton Division stretching from the Chester City boundary as far as Farndon on the Welsh border. The superintendent seated wearing the braided tunic is Edward Charles Hicks, who joined the force in 1879. Broxton Division was absorbed into the Chester City Division in 1949, following the merger with the city force. (Museum collection)

Sergeant William Ratcliffe (sitting) with two colleagues pictured around 1904 when stationed at Nantwich. He joined the force in 1888 after service in the 12th Lancers and retired in 1914. The shako worn for normal duty was unique to the Cheshire force and continued to be worn until 1935. (Museum collection)

The Macclesfield force photographed in 1903 on the retirement of Chief Constable William Sheasby (seated centre in civilian clothes). He was appointed chief constable in 1874 having previously served in the Coventry force as a detective inspector. In 1882, he sustained serious injury when an attempt was made on his life by a man armed with a knife; his attacker was apprehended and later sentenced to penal servitude for life. (*History of the Macclesfield Borough Police* by C.C. Symonds, 1947)

Sergeant Thomas Jackson with his wife and children outside his police cottage at Gawsworth around 1905. A native of Lymm, he had joined the force in 1881 after five years' service in the 2nd Battalion, 8th Regiment of Foot (Liverpool Regiment). In the photograph he is wearing his 2nd Afghan War Medal (1878–80). His elder son Percy (right) was to lose his life in the First World War. (Peter Barton)

PC Samuel Gilchrist of the Warrington Borough force seen here, in 1903, driving the first Warrington police car, a Sunbeam. The car was loaned by a local motor dealer for use by the force. PC Gilchrist was born in Ireland in 1876, joined the force in 1899, serving until 1911, when he retired on grounds of ill health. The identity of the passengers is unknown. (Museum collection)

Sergeant Frank Williams joined the force in 1893 and was posted to Dukinfield. He is pictured here around 1905 outside St Luke's parish church, in the centre of Holmes Chapel where he was stationed at the time. He retired in 1920; his conduct during his service is recorded as 'exemplary'. (Museum collection)

Members of the Eddisbury Division pictured around 1905 outside Oakmere Police Station, which also served as divisional headquarters covering a large area of rural Cheshire, including Frodsham and Tarporley. The young man wearing civilian clothes is thought to be a recruit having yet to be issued with his uniform. This former station, located on the main A556 Chester–Manchester road, although still in existence, is sadly in a semi-derelict state. (Museum collection)

Albert Sudlow is pictured when he was a sergeant at Tarporley, between 1906 and 1909. Sudlow was born in 1871 at Ellesmere in Shropshire, and joined the force in 1893, having previously worked as a boilermaker at Crewe railway works. He retired in 1930 when he was the superintendent in charge of the Stockport Division. (Museum Collection)

Members of the Crewe Section (*c.* 1905) pictured in the rear yard of the police station at Edleston Road. The young boy in the foreground is probably the son of one of the officers. The station was built in 1876 and closed in 1939 when the convent at Nantwich Road was adapted to become the Crewe Divisional Headquarters and Police Station. The former station at Edleston Road was demolished in the 1950s. (Museum collection)

Members of the Nantwich Division (*c.* 1910). Seated second from right, wearing his Boer War campaign medals, is Acting Sergeant Herbert Dodd who was stationed at Barbridge. A total of nineteen Cheshire officers were recalled for military service in the Boer War, the officer standing far left, middle row is also wearing medals awarded for service in that conflict. (Keith Foster)

The police cottage at Barbridge near Nantwich around 1912, which was occupied by Herbert Dodd and his family. A metal plaque bearing the force crest is affixed to the wall and a noticeboard displaying official posters can be seen in the garden. The young girl in the photograph holding a doll is Herbert's daughter, Elsie, who was 8 years of age at the time. (Keith Foster)

Superintendent Thomas Henry Garner is pictured here in his gig with his wife Emma in 1911, when he was in charge of Nantwich Division. Superintendents received a horse allowance of £55 per annum to cover all costs. Gradually, as motor transport evolved, some superintendents acquired cars instead for which a similar allowance was paid, with horse allowance ceasing altogether in 1923. (Museum collection)

An inspector and two constables of the Chester City force (*c.* 1910). The photograph is thought to have been taken on the Roodee, where skaters and children are enjoying the icy conditions. Whether the officers are assisting the skater to remain upright or taking him into custody is not known! (Museum collection)

Cheshire officers pictured outside Eccleston Police Station (*c.* 1910). Part of their duties would have included dealing with matters occurring on the Grosvenor Estate, such as poaching, as well as providing a police presence at important events held at Eaton Hall – the country house of the Duke of Westminster. Constable James Thelwell, who was stationed at Pulford, is standing on the far right. The former police station is now a private residence. (Maurice Titmuss)

Constable Abram Jones joined the force in 1888 after eleven months' service in the Salford police. He initially served in the Wirral Division, but spent most of his later service in the Crewe area. The merit badge worn above his good conduct stripe had been awarded to him in 1908 for 'long and meritorious service'. It also entitled him to 2*d* per day additional pay. He retired in 1919. (Museum collection)

A copy of the certificate of character and service issued to Abraham Jones upon his retirement from the force in 1919. (Museum collection)

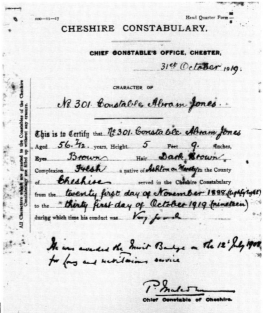

Northwich Division officers photographed outside Northwich Police Station, in Brockhurst Street (*c.* 1910). Magistrates' Courts, or Police Courts as they were commonly known, were often housed above the station, as was the case at Northwich. A notice giving details of court sittings can be seen to the left of the door. The building was demolished in the early 1970s to make way for a new court building. (Museum collection)

A constable of the Warrington Borough force, around 1910, taking a break from patrol. The helmet beside him on the seat is made of straw. The straw helmet first came to prominence in the Luton force around 1903, and was later adopted by several forces for wear during summer months, as they were light and reflected sunlight much better than the traditional heavier helmet. (Museum collection)

Brothers Thomas and Edward Price pictured with their mother, Jane, around 1912. Both served in the Chester City force. Thomas (right) joined in 1902 and Edward in 1911. In 1915, Edward enlisted in the 1st Battalion Coldstream Guards, and on 20 November 1917, he was killed in action on the first day of the Battle of Cambrai. Thomas retired as a sergeant in 1933 and died in 1941. (Cheshire Archives & Local Studies)

Men of the Cheshire Constabulary lead the funeral cortège of former Chief Superintendent John Hindley, en route to Wallasey Crematorium in 1911. John Hindley was held in high esteem by members of the force during his time in command at Wallasey. He continued to reside in the area after his retirement in 1899. (Museum collection)

Members of the force pictured outside Chester Castle on 16 August 1912, following the presentation of 1911 Coronation Medals by Colonel France-Hayhurst, Chairman of the Standing Joint Committee (seated centre). Seated to his right is Colonel Hammersley, the former chief constable (1881–1910) and to his left Colonel Pulteney Malcolm, the chief constable at the time. Wearing the cap is William Leah, Deputy Chief Constable, who is standing immediately behind Colonel France-Hayhurst. (Museum collection)

Sergeant Robert Smith was born in Lambeth and joined the Chester City force in 1890. The white helmet seen on the side table was adopted by the force in 1915, to be worn with the summer uniform. Several other forces, particularly in some of the holiday resorts, adopted similar headgear. The Isle of Man Constabulary is the only force still to wear white helmets in the summer months. (Michael Hunt)

James Herbert Price is pictured here in 1914 just after he had joined the Warrington force. Price enlisted in the armed forces in 1915, returned to the police force in 1919 and was promoted to sergeant in 1929. Sadly, he died in service in 1931. The ornate nature of the Warrington helmet and badge can be seen in this photograph. (Museum collection)

Ernest James Thelwell joined the Cheshire force in March 1913 and served at Dukinfield and Bramhall, before enlisting in the Grenadier Guards during the First World War. He was killed in action at Gommecourt on the Somme in September 1916, aged 25 years. His father James Thelwall served in the Cheshire Constabulary between 1886 and 1913, retiring within a few months of his son joining the force. (Maurice Titmuss)

Members of the 2nd Battalion (Birkenhead) Cheshire Volunteer Regiment pictured in 1917, with members of the Birkenhead Borough force. The soldiers were attested as special constables to assist in the policing of the Royal National Eisteddfod of Wales held in Birkenhead Park. The event passed off in an orderly manner without incident and their services were not necessary. (Museum collection)

In 1917, the Birkenhead force, with a depleted strength due to officers serving in the armed forces, recruited twelve female officers, two of whom are pictured here. At the end of the war, many of these officers left the service and, by 1920, only three remained. The remaining three all later resigned after applying for parity in pay with their male colleagues, which was refused. (*Maintaining the Queen's Peace*, 1958)

Colonel Pulteney Malcolm CBE DSO MVO served as Cheshire's chief constable between 1910 and 1934. Born in India in 1861 the son of a general, he had served in the army until 1904 and had received the Albert Medal for Gallantry (third medal from left in the photograph). During the First World War, he returned to the army whilst his deputy Superintendent William Leah took command of the force. (Museum collection)

3

POLICING BETWEEN THE WARS

PC David Evans performing point duty at Birkenhead in the early 1920s. He grew up in Bala, North Wales, and worked as a miner before joining the Birkenhead Borough force in 1919. During his final years of service, he studied and gained a degree in theology and was ordained when he retired from the force in 1944. (Cheshire Constabulary)

Arthur Sandland pictured about 1920
when superintendent at Wallasey.
He joined the county force in 1899 from
the Cheshire Regiment, and within three
months was recalled to serve in the Boer
War. He rejoined the force in 1902 and
by 1913 was a sergeant at Liscard, when
he transferred to the new Wallasey force.
His son Charles followed him into that
force in 1919 and rose to become deputy
chief constable in 1952. (*History of
Wallasey Borough Police* by Noel Smith)

A constable of the Hyde Borough
force in the 1920s, pictured
with staff outside the servants'
lodge of Hyde Hall, the home of
the Ashton family. The inverted
chevrons on the officer's right
sleeve are good conduct stripes
for which he would be rewarded
with a few pence per day extra
pay. (Museum collection)

Superintendent John Lees (seated centre) around 1925, with his inspectors and sergeants when he was in command of the Altrincham Division. Superintendent Lees served in the Cheshire force for forty-four years, retiring aged 65 in 1936. The photograph was taken at the rear of Altrincham Town Hall. (Museum collection)

Superintendent Albert Sudlow (seated centre) with officers of the Hazel Grove Section of the Stockport Division, in 1926. Detective Sergeant Alfred Weatherby in homburg, seated to the left of the group, went on to become a chief superintendent and was in charge of the North-East Cheshire Division when he retired in 1954. The Stockport Division was absorbed into the Dukinfield Division in 1934. (Museum collection)

PC William Shepherd pictured with the family of the local coal merchant at Bollington during the 1920s. He had joined the force in July 1914 and seen service in the armed forces during the First World War. He retired in 1946 when serving in the Wirral Division. (Clive Haycocks)

PC John Barr seen here performing point duty at Market Gate, Warrington in the 1920s. He is standing on a heavy duty rubber mat in the centre of the road, which ensures he will maintain his position. (Museum collection)

Sergeant Thomas Latham is pictured here in the uniform of the Wallasey Borough force. He originally joined the Cheshire Constabulary in 1907 after serving in the North Staffordshire Regiment. In 1913, whilst stationed at New Brighton, he opted to transfer to the newly created Wallasey force. He is seen here wearing the King and Queen's South Africa medals awarded for his service in the Boer War. (Nick Latham)

During the General Strike of 1926, a detachment of Warrington officers (pictured) were sent to Wigan to assist the local force. Inspector Green (seated centre) was in command of the Warrington contingent. Superintendent Gordon of the Wigan force is seated to his right and Mr T. Pey, Chief Constable of Wigan, to his left. (Museum collection)

The Stockport Borough Police photographed in 1926. The force had been formed in 1870, and by 1967 it had grown to a strength of just under 300 officers. At this point, it was amalgamated and became 'H' Division of the Cheshire Constabulary. In 1974, Stockport and the surrounding former Cheshire area became 'J' Division of the Greater Manchester Police. (Museum collection)

There have been a number of instances where several members of the same family have served in the force. Walter Spann (pictured) joined the Cheshire Constabulary in 1921 after military service in the First World War, and was later to be followed into the force by two brothers. He remained a constable throughout his service and retired in 1946 when stationed at Runcorn. (Alan Spann)

Walter's brother Frederick (pictured) joined the force in 1925 at Winsford. He also remained a constable throughout his service and retired at Weaverham in 1954. His son, Alan Spann, also joined the force in 1957, later retiring as an inspector in Greater Manchester Police. (Alan Spann)

The third Spann brother Philip (pictured) joined the force in 1930 at Altrincham. He was later promoted to sergeant. He resigned in 1945 to pursue a career with the Shell Oil Company, where he became a senior security manager at the Stanlow site. The top arm badge denotes he holds a St John Ambulance certificate in first aid and the lower badge denotes a Royal Life Saving Association qualification. (Alan Spann)

Prior to the 1974 local government boundary changes, Widnes had always been policed by the Lancashire Constabulary, which had been formed in 1839. This photograph showing members of the Widnes Division was taken about 1925 in the rear yard of Widnes Police Station, then situated in Victoria Road. (Museum collection)

The police station at George Lane, Bredbury (c. 1925). The officers pictured include Inspector Murdoch McKenzie Thorburn, a native of Dundee who was in charge at Bredbury between 1922 and 1927. The police station, which was built in 1900, provided separate living accommodation for both the inspector and sergeant. The women and children pictured are thought to be family members of both officers. (Museum collection)

This smart group of Warrington Borough officers (*c.* 1930) are parading for the annual inspection by His Majesty's Inspector of Constabulary. It is clear from the campaign medals worn that quite a number of these officers had seen military service in the First World War. Their personal equipment, including a greatcoat, cape and truncheon are laid out for inspection. (Museum collection)

Henry Sheasby, seen here in full dress uniform, was the chief constable of Macclesfield between 1907 and 1942. He joined the Cheshire Constabulary in 1893 and rose to the rank of inspector at Crewe, before his appointment to the Macclesfield force. He was the second Sheasby to have been Macclesfield's chief constable; his father, William, held the post between 1874 and 1903. (Museum collection)

The year 1930 saw a new approach by central government to the question of motor traffic, resulting in the Road Traffic Act of 1930. The Act also provided a 100 per cent grant to aid forces in the formation of police motor patrols. In Cheshire, a number of AJS motorcycle combinations were purchased to patrol the roads of the county. (Museum collection)

An officer attending the scene of a road accident in High Street, Sandbach, in the early 1930s. Details of the incident are unknown but a pedal cycle appears to be trapped under the lorry. The Road Traffic Act of 1930 was introduced to regulate traffic on the roads and the use of motor vehicles; it also introduced the requirement for third party insurance. (Museum collection)

A street scene in Stockton Heath, around 1930. A lorry owned by Stotherts of John Street, Warrington, manufacturers of carbonated drinks, has shed its load. A police constable is on hand to direct operations during the clean-up. Whether or not the driver was prosecuted for having an insecure load is unknown. (Museum collection)

Warrington Borough force photographed around 1930 outside Arpley Street Police Station. The strength of the force at that time was just over 100 officers. Chief Constable Martin Nicholls is seated to the mayor's right; he served as chief constable between 1907 and 1937, having previously served in the Reading Borough force and as chief constable of Windsor. Following retirement, he continued as commandant of the Warrington Special Constabulary. (Museum collection)

Wallasey Borough Police transport section lined up for a force inspection (*c.* 1930). The vehicle furthest from the camera has a large spotlight mounted on the roof, the various makes of the vehicles in the photograph are unknown, but, no doubt, some readers will be able to identify them. (Museum collection)

This photograph captures officers of the Warrington Borough force (*c.* 1930) marching from the police station at Arpley Street en route to their beats. This was a common practice in many borough and city forces at the time; the sergeant would march with the column and detail each man on arrival at his designated beat. (Museum collection)

The funeral cortége of Mr John Danby, Chief Constable of Hyde, being led by members of the borough force as it passes along Market Street in 1931. Danby had served as chief constable since Hyde had become an independent force in 1899, and later achieved some measure of distinction as the founder of the very successful Hyde Lads Club, who used the former police station premises in Beeley Street for many years. (Museum collection)

In 1932, Constable Alfred Cleaver (pictured) and Sergeant Capper of the Chester City force rescued several persons from a blazing house in Trinity Street. Both officers were later awarded the medal of the Royal Humane Society, and Constable Cleaver, for additional risk, received the King's Police Medal for Gallantry and the Bronze Medal for the Protection of Life from Fire; he retired as an inspector in 1953. (Museum collection)

Constable Samuel Jones at the wheel of an MG Magnette sports car in about 1934. The force inaugurated a 'courtesy cop' or special scheme in an attempt to reduce road deaths and this vehicle was one of several assorted types used to patrol the major roads of the county. Over the period of the scheme road deaths were drastically reduced. (Museum collection)

With the increase in road traffic during the early 1930s, police forces needed to keep pace and introduced motor patrols. The Metropolitan Police opened a driving school in 1934 and Cheshire quickly seized on this development and sent officers for training. Officers attending this course in early 1935 included four from Cheshire, distinctive by the shako badge on their caps. (Museum collection)

During the 1930s, the Chester City force provided a network of ten police boxes, each with a telephone linked to the police station for use by police or the public. The one pictured was situated at Grosvenor Road. Officers on the beat could be alerted by the flashing light, and the interior could be used for report writing and meal breaks. (Cheshire Archives and Local Studies)

PC Thomas Elwin (pictured) joined the force in 1933. The helmet he is wearing was traditionally worn on special occasions; the Prince of Wales' Feathers are embodied in the wreath-shape helmet badge and the belt fastening is similarly adorned. The helmet and the shako were abolished in 1935 in favour of caps, which were routinely worn until 1964 when the combed-style helmets currently worn by the force were introduced. (Museum collection)

Adam Graham left the family farm in Hawick in the Scottish Borders in 1935 and travelled south to join the Stalybridge Borough Police, which then numbered thirty-five officers. Following the 1947 amalgamation, he continued to serve at Stalybridge and retired as a sergeant in 1963. The unusual trim around the collar of his tunic, which can be seen in the photograph, was an adornment adopted by the Stalybridge force. (Bill Graham)

By the mid-1930s, the force had purchased several different makes of vehicle for driver training and patrol duties. The Humber saloon pictured was acquired in January 1936. Other vehicles used by the force included a Chrysler Straight 8, Alvis 27hp, MG Magnette 18hp, Riley 14hp, Standard 20hp and a Triumph. (Museum collection)

The Congleton force photographed in 1935. At this time its strength, including the chief constable, was thirteen, which remained the same until 1947 when the force was amalgamated with the Cheshire Constabulary. Chief Constable R.W. James (seated centre) became a superintendent in Cheshire and later wrote the force history titled *To the Best of our Skill and Knowledge: A Short History of the Cheshire Constabulary, 1857-1957* to coincide the 100th anniversary in 1957. (Museum collection)

Hyde Borough Police photographed in 1935. Formed in 1899 it remained an independent force until 1947, when it was merged with Cheshire. Four officers in the photograph wearing caps and open-necked tunics (two sergeants seated far left and two constables, second and rear rows) are members of the fire brigade section of the force. Seated centre is Chief Constable William Smith MM. (Museum collection)

Major Jack Becke, Chief Constable of Cheshire (1935–46), with his family. The golden Labrador in the photograph was a stray that he had adopted and was often to be seen at his side at police functions. Shortly after taking command, he abolished the shako hat in favour of caps. He was knighted in 1944. (Museum collection)

Recruits pictured in late 1939 before wartime restrictions on recruitment of regular officers came into effect. Seated fourth from left is Arthur Morris, who became a chief superintendent. Constable Bob Weighill (centre row, far right) volunteered for the RAF in 1941 and became a fighter pilot. He did not return to the force after the war, instead making a career in the RAF and eventually rising to air commodore. (Museum collection)

4

WARTIME POLICING

Mr John Ormerod, Chief Constable of Wallasey, pictured with Lord Derby in September 1940 at the opening of a new extension to Wallasey Police Station. PC Hugh Henderson, to the left, had joined the force in 1931 and he later volunteered for RAF aircrew and served as a flight engineer in Bomber Command, attaining the rank of flying officer. He was lost in action over Germany in March 1945. (Museum collection)

Right: During the 1930s, Cheshire recruited heavily from the armed forces particularly the Guards Brigade. Following the outbreak of hostilities in September 1939, a total of 104 officers with reserve obligations were recalled to the colours and in November a parade of those officers took place on the forecourt of Chester Castle. Chief Constable Jack Becke is seen here, accompanied by his Labrador, Alice, speaking with one of the officers during his inspection. (Museum collection)

Left: The chief constable reviews the march past. Twelve of these men were to lose their lives in the war, whilst others gained commissions, awards and high commendations. At the time, the strength of the force was under 800, and the loss of 104 experienced officers at one stroke had a significant impact, although the recruitment of large numbers of special constables and the recall of police reservists helped. (Museum collection)

Road accidents involving pedestrians increased during wartime due to the blackout. To highlight awareness the Birkenhead force formed an Accident Prevention Section and equipped their patrol cars, pictured, with placards carrying a road safety message and advice. It is not known how effective the tactic was in reducing accidents. (Museum collection)

Pictured is the mobile canteen and soup kitchen operated by the Special Constabulary (*c.* 1941) as part of the county ARP organisation. The vehicle was used at the scene of bomb devastation and other major incidents. Members of the Cheshire force together with elements of the borough forces formed part of the Regional Police Reserve, which were sent to assist the Liverpool City Police during the heavy raids of late 1941. (Museum collection)

This Armstrong Sideley ARP ambulance is pictured outside Bromborough Police Station (*c.* 1941). Wartime adaptations can be seen: note the large, white circle painted above the cab, together with white-painted bumper bar and edges of mudguards, and running board all done to try to make it more visible to other road users during blackouts. The hooded headlamp was also another wartime requirement. (Museum collection)

Damage caused to the police garages at Bromborough Divisional Headquarters during a raid on 16 September 1940 – the bomb crater can be clearly seen. During late 1940 and early 1941 there were several heavy raids targeting the Mersey docks systems. In one particular raid in Bebbington alone, on the night of 12 March and into the morning of 13 March 1941, twenty-four persons were killed and about 110 injured. (Museum collection)

On 8 October 1940, a German JU88 bomber crash landed on land at Bromborough Dock (pictured) having been shot down by pilots of a Czech squadron based at Speke. A police officer can be seen together with a member of the armed forces guarding the aircraft. One member of the four-man crew was killed. (Museum collection)

In this photograph, a police officer makes notes in his pocketbook, whilst speaking with a local resident amongst the rubble of demolished dwellings on the Stanton Estate at Lower Bebbington, following a raid on 23 November 1940. (Museum collection)

On the night of 7 April 1941, sixteen high-explosive bombs and a large number of incendiaries were dropped on the Earle Street area of Crewe, demolishing eleven houses and damaging over 300. Pictured is the devastation in Martin Street where a direct hit demolished a surface air-raid shelter. A total of sixteen people, including Constable Frank Marshall who was on night duty, were killed during the raid. (Museum collection)

Constable Frank Marshall joined the Cheshire Constabulary in August 1938 and was posted to Crewe. He was a single man and a native of Wilmslow, and at the time of his death, on 8 April 1941, he was 24 years of age. He is buried at St John's church in Wilmslow. (*Wilmslow Advertiser*)

A police sergeant standing in a bomb crater at the rear of houses in Town Lane, Bebbington following a raid on 1 November 1941. The crater caused by a heavy calibre bomb measured 57ft wide and 17ft deep. A number of people had to be dug out of their homes and Anderson shelters in their gardens, miraculously there was not one single casualty. (Museum collection)

WARNING

BY THE DEFENCE REGULATIONS

A PERSON CONVICTED OF

LOOTING

IS LIABLE TO BE SENTENCED TO

DEATH

OR TO PENAL SERVITUDE FOR

LIFE.

County Constabulary,
Chester.   23. 12 40.

J. BECKE.
Chief Constable of Cheshire.

'A grim warning' – posters warning of the consequences of looting were introduced throughout the country during the Second World War: this is an example of the one issued by the chief constable of Cheshire. The number of cases dealt with in Cheshire under this wartime legislation is unknown. During the first eight weeks of the London Blitz, there were 390 cases of looting reported to the police. (Museum collection)

In the summer of 1941, King George VI and Queen Elizabeth visited Crewe to inspect representative sections of the county Air Raid Precautions and allied organisations who paraded at Crewe Alexandra football ground. They are seen here being welcomed by Chief Constable Jack Becke with a police guard of honour; the white cap covers had been introduced before the war. (Museum collection)

Officers of the Hoylake Section, headed by Sergeant Charles Mort, march past the Council Offices in Market Street, Hoylake, on VE Day in 1945. During the war, special constables, war reserve constables and officers who had been brought out of retirement supplemented the depleted force in considerable numbers. (Gerry Mort)

5

POST-WAR POLICING

Pictured are the first female police officers appointed by Cheshire in 1946. Some had seen service in the WAPC (Women's Auxiliary Police Corp) during the war. Edith Allen (seated centre) was later to become one the first female detective constables in the force and she retired as a sergeant in 1967. Alice Beatty (standing, second from left) served at Hyde for many years; she retired in 1971. (Museum collection)

Pictured are some of the first officers to be trained at No. 1 District Police Training Centre, Bruche, Warrington, in 1946. On the right of the photograph in the forefront is PC Harold Foulkes and immediately behind him is PC Len Jones, both of the Warrington force. Harold Foulkes later became a superintendent and Len Jones a sergeant. Students had to take down detailed notes of all lectures in longhand. (Museum collection)

Before the Underwater Search Unit was established in the late 1960s, searching waterways for bodies or discarded items such as firearms or stolen property was a 'hit and miss' affair. In serious cases, waterways such as canals could be drained. This photograph, taken on the Bridgewater Canal at Lymm in the early 1950s, shows officers using grappling hooks to scour the canal bed. (Margaret Chambers)

Constable Clifford Woodcock, pictured when stationed at Winsford in the early 1950s. Woodcock joined the force in 1938 and enlisted for army service in 1942, serving in the South Lancashire Regiment and later being commissioned as a captain. Returning to the force in 1945, he rose through the ranks to become an assistant chief constable; he was awarded the Queen's Police Medal in 1975 and retired from the force the following year. (Museum collection)

Sergeant John Allman instructing students attending a driving course (*c.* 1950) on the rudiments of vehicle maintenance. All vehicle servicing and repairs of police vehicles was undertaken at the Central Garages at Crewe, and officers attending from division with a vehicle for service were required to don overalls and assist the mechanic. (Museum collection)

Police were responsible for the destruction of the carcases of cattle infected with contagious diseases, such as anthrax. This photograph, taken in the early 1950s, shows flame guns being prepared for use on a farm in the county. The man wearing overalls is a mechanic from the police garages at Crewe, who were responsible for the maintenance and use of the equipment. (Museum collection)

The flame guns are in use in this picture, the carcass has been placed in a pit and the remains will be buried following destruction. The burners were fuelled by gas. (Museum collection)

One of the two specially constructed mobile canteens that were introduced in 1950 to provide refreshment for officers engaged at the scene of a major event or incident. The catering staff worked in cramped conditions, but were able to provide anything from sandwiches to hot meals, including dessert and frequent cups of tea, as seen here. (Museum collection)

Constable Douglas Gardiner beside his Rover 12 patrol car (c. 1952). Rover cars were used by the force for motor patrol duties in the post-war years until 1965, when they were replaced with Ford Zephyrs. The Cheshire Rover patrol cars were distinctive by their green colour; it is unclear why the force adopted green when most other forces opted for black. (Museum collection)

Members of Warrington Borough CID parading for inspection by Her Majesty's Inspector of Constabulary in the early 1950s. The trilby hat was required headgear for detectives in those days. Detective Inspector Arthur Galbraith is standing nearest the camera with Detective Sergeant George Welborn standing to his right. (Museum collection)

In 1953, a contingent of over 100 Cheshire officers did duty in the Mall during the Coronation of Queen Elizabeth II. The officers were accommodated in tents erected in Hyde Park, as can be seen by this group of officers standing beside their tent. (Museum collection)

The contingent of Cheshire policewomen who attended the Royal Review of the Police in 1954. Pictured from left: PCs Hamer and Williams, Sergeant Welburn, PCs Dow and Riley. Helen Welburn later retired from the force in the rank of superintendent and Mildred Dow as a chief superintendent in the Greater Manchester Police. (Museum collection)

Constable Len Wadcock, one of the first Cheshire officers trained as a dog handler, photographed in 1954 with his dog, Niko, prior to attending the Royal Review of the Police in London. The Dog Section was formed in 1951 and selected officers were trained at the Surrey Police Dog Training School at Mount Browne. Handlers were based in divisions and equipped with specially converted cars for transporting their dogs. (Museum collection)

The contingent from the Warrington Borough force who attended the Royal Review of the Police held in London in July 1954. Standing from left: PCs Coope, Genge, Inman, Unsworth, Greig, Jones and Wells. Seated from left: PCs Smyth, Harman and Sergeant Taylor, Chief Inspector Walker, Special Sergeant Woodward and PCs Wallace and Lucas. Over 10,000 officers drawn from all forces in the United Kingdom attended the parade. (Museum collection)

Constable Les Clarke of the Stockport Borough force pictured in around 1955 with a Wolseley patrol car – no 'blues and twos' in those days, but note the loudspeaker mounted on the front bumper. The photograph was taken at the rear of the old Theatre Royal, Petersgate, where the police garages were located. (Gwilym Williams)

Constable Bill Holland of Headquarters Fingerprint Department pictured in the 1950s, checking an outstanding fingerprint from the scene of a crime against a set of prints from the files. This was painstaking work for the fingerprint expert who was required to match sixteen points of similarity before the evidence could be used in court. (Museum collection)

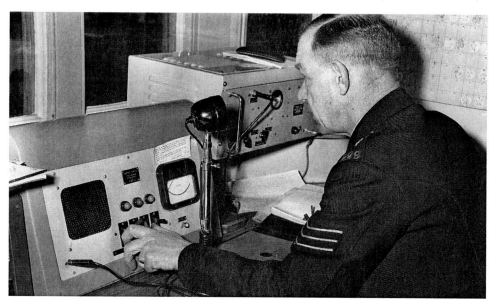

Sergeant Kenneth Lakin, seen here in 1955, operating the force radio communication system in the information room at the police headquarters in Foregate Street, Chester. Compared with present technology the system was quite basic, but served its purpose in maintaining radio communication with vehicles on patrol. (Museum collection)

In the 1950s, American military aircraft were flying from Burtonwood to the North Pole to forecast weather conditions, and local children decided to utilise this service as a way of getting their letters delivered to Santa. The American forces magazine *Stars and Stripes* featured the story and this photograph of Warrington PC Cyril Lamerick assisting one child to post her letter appeared in the magazine. (Angela Lamerick)

Members of the Police Dog Section pictured about 1955 training in Delamere Forest. Standing, from left to right: Sergeant Len Wadcock, constables Bob Taylor with Olaf, George Booth (Beta), Peter Dainty (Nora), Roy Suckley (Ajax), Tony Ratledge (Wenna), Ian Halbert (Niko) and Frank Argent (Pablo). They were stationed in divisions performing CID duties in addition to their role as dog handlers. (Cheshire Constabulary)

Staff of the Driving School based at Crewe with some members of Crewe Division motor patrol section pictured in 1957, with two of the green Rover 75 patrol cars used by the force at the time. The Driving School originally opened in 1937 at Hoole, but closed for the duration of the war and reopened at Crewe in 1948. Several other forces also sent officers for training at the school. (Museum collection)

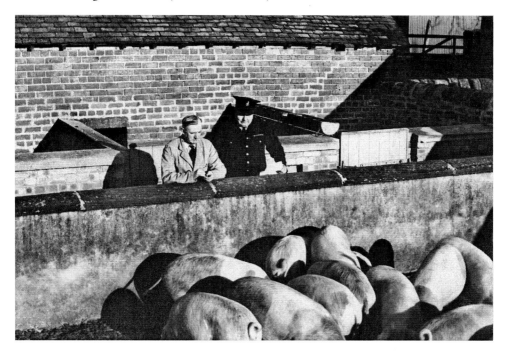

Constable Arthur Laurinson, pictured in 1956, checking pig licences at a farm on his rural beat at Alpraham, near Tarporley. Police had the duty of enforcing legislation in relation to diseases of animals and, in the case of swine fever, they were responsible for issuing licences for the movement of pigs in infected areas. (Museum collection)

Members of the Bredbury, Marple and Mellor sections pictured (above) in 1957 at the rear of Bredbury Police Station. The photograph was taken to mark the occasion of the retirement of Assistant Chief Constable George Durnell (seated fourth from left). Sitting to his right is Chief Superintendent Barney O'Sullivan, the officer in command of the North East Cheshire Division at the time. (Museum collection)

'Shaking hands with door handles.' This constable in the 1950s is pictured (above) at night checking lock-up premises on his beat. Insecure premises and unusual lights had to be reported and on occasions, villains would be caught in the act of breaking in by the patrolling officer. (Museum collection)

Two Cheshire officers seen here dealing with a serious road traffic accident during the 1950s. They are taking measurements to try to establish the cause of the collision in order for a full report to be compiled for consideration of any necessary further action. (Museum collection)

The Stockport Police Band pictured marching along Petersgate, Stockport, on Mayor's Sunday (c. 1960). PC Gwilym Williams is playing the baritone, second from left, with PC Ron Clayton immediately behind. PC Ron Shawcross with side drum is at the rear of the column. (Gwilym Williams)

Stockport Borough Police Band pictured in the mid-1950s. The band was formed in 1952, and on amalgamation in 1967 became the Cheshire Constabulary Band, which continues to the present day. The senior officers of the force (centre front, left to right) are Superintendent Cyril Hirst, Chief Constable William Rees and Chief Inspector Tom Walker. The bandmaster, Constable Charles Holt, is far left (front). (Gwilym Williams)

A Crewe policewoman seen reassuring a young child (c. 1959). The role of females in the service had traditionally been concerned with matters involving women and children. Following the introduction of equal opportunities legislation in the early 1970s this changed, and for the first time female officers received the same level of pay and performed the same duties as their male colleagues. (Museum collection)

The Stockport Borough Police vehicle fleet in 1959, with newly acquired Vauxhall Velox patrol cars (forefront) together with a plain Vauxhall Wyvern CID car and Bedford general purpose van (behind). The photograph was taken in Woodbank Park. (Gwilym Williams)

6

THE SIXTIES AND SEVENTIES

PC Ben Halfpenny of the Warrington force seen here leading elephants from Bank Quay Station, where they had arrived by train, along Parker Street to the circus ground at Victoria Park. The photograph is believed to have been taken in the late 1950s or early '60s. (Margaret Halfpenny)

This large camera was used in the photographic department at headquarters to capture images for use in police publications. It was purchased in the mid-1940s and remained in daily use until the new headquarters opened in 1967. The camera was moved along the track to enable the lens to focus on the material to be photographed. (Museum collection)

Sergeant Danny Hanberry and PC Joe Crookes lead the Walking Day procession through Warrington town centre in around 1960. Walking Day has its origins in the early nineteenth century and is traditionally a religious procession with a carnival atmosphere held every summer. The police are kept busy with hundreds of people thronging the streets of Warrington to take part in the festivities. (Museum collection)

Four officers pictured at this Commendation Parade in 1963 received bravery awards for their part in the arrest of two men at Macclesfield armed with a sawn-off shotgun. Detective Sergeant Ken Etchells (seated far left) and Detective Constable Norman Dawson (seated sixth from left) were both awarded the British Empire Medal for Gallantry, constables Stan Smith (second left, middle row) and Mike Bell (fifth left, middle row) both received the Queen's Commendation for Brave Conduct. During the incident, nitric acid was thrown over the officers and a police dog was so badly injured that it had to be destroyed. (Museum collection)

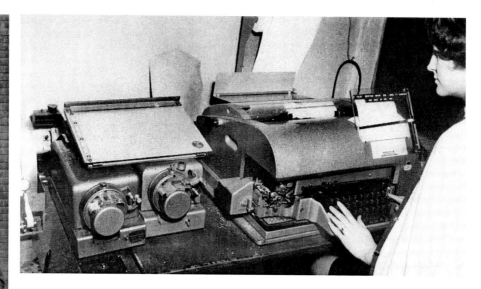

Before the advent of the computer and email communication, circulations from headquarters to divisions, and vice versa, was by teleprinter. Pictured is a female staff member at the Foregate Street Headquarters in the early 1960s, operating the equipment. Only the Divisional Headquarters had teleprinter facilities and messages were passed on to sections by telephone and details recorded in long hand. (Museum collection)

Her Majesty's Inspector of Constabulary, Sir Charles Martin speaking with Sergeant Ernie Pocock during a government inspection at Bromborough around 1962. Looking on is Chief Superintendent Joe Hawkes. In 1941, Sergeant Pocock, then a constable, and Constable Frank Wiggins attended the scene of a crashed Wellington Bomber near Church Minshull and attempted to rescue the crew amid exploding ammunition; they were both later awarded the British Empire Medal for Gallantry. (Museum collection)

In the early 1960s, the Stockport Borough force introduced courtesy patrols equipped with distinctively marked Morris Minor saloons. The idea of the scheme was to advise motorists where poor driving habits had been witnessed and also where minor traffic infringements had been committed as an alternative to prosecution. Pictured from left: PCs Hughie Hulme, Fred Fearnley, Tom Barrow and Geoff Davies. (*Stockport News* Photo Service)

PC Ron Stockton astride a BSA A65 650cc twin motorcycle in 1964; these were the first traffic patrol motorcycles to be brought into use by the Cheshire force. The photograph was taken at Knutsford services on the M6. (Museum collection)

Cadets of the Chester City and Headquarters Divisions marching through Chester in May 1963 to take part in a parade with other youth organisations, in order to mark Commonwealth Youth Sunday. Cadets joined from the age of 16 and received training in various aspects of police work, with a view to becoming constables at the age of 19. The single stripe denotes the rank of head cadet, which carried an increase in pay of 1/-d per week. (Bill Havers)

In 1964, courses of one month's duration were introduced for police cadets, which were held at the training centre at Crewe. Pictured are cadets attending one of these early courses where instruction included general police procedures, law and foot drill. The instructors seated from left: Constable Bill Smith, Sergeant Jack Dyas, Chief Inspector Denis Bailey and Constable Jones. (Museum collection)

The Mellor Section, seen here with their Vellocette motorcycles, are being inspected by Chief Constable Henry Watson in 1964. The machines were ideal for the hilly terrain the officers were required to patrol, although when first introduced in 1963 the officers were not issued with any protective clothing or a helmet. The chief constable is seen here speaking to Constable Alan Suett. (Alan Suett)

Ford Zephyr Mark III Estates were the first cars used to patrol the M6 in 1964. The motorway opened in 1963 and the following year an experimental joint unit was formed, comprising officers from Staffordshire, Cheshire and Lancashire to police the whole stretch of the M6 in being at that time. The experiment lasted for five months and provided many useful lessons in this new aspect of traffic policing. (Cheshire Constabulary)

Superintendent Bill Wills of the Runcorn Division, accompanied by Chief Inspector Siebert Williams, inspects a divisional parade at Runcorn in August 1965. These parades were held at least annually in each division when performance and efficiency were scrutinised by the superintendent in charge. (Museum collection)

In August 1966, 10-year-old Jane Elizabeth Taylor disappeared from Mobberley. A large-scale search was mounted in the local area. Pictured are detectives utilising farm machinery in the search for clues. In 1975, Jane's remains were discovered buried in North Wales and a man was arrested and convicted of abducting and murdering her. (Margaret Chambers)

On 6 September 1966, 650 officers representing every division and department marched from the castle to Chester Cathedral for a memorial service to honour three Metropolitan police officers, who had been shot dead at Shepherds Bush on 12 August. The procession was headed by the Stockport Borough Police Band. In this photograph, the parade is seen marching along Bridge Street towards the cathedral. (Cheshire Constabulary)

The policewomen's contingent arriving at the cathedral to take part in the memorial service for the three murdered officers. (Cheshire Constabulary)

Senior detective officers of the force headed by Detective Chief Superintendent Arthur Benfield marching to Chester Cathedral to attend the memorial service for their fallen colleagues. (Margaret Chambers)

A policewoman seeing children safely across Nantwich Road, Crewe, on their way to school in 1967. Officers were detailed daily for school crossing duty before school crossing patrol wardens, commonly known as 'lollipop ladies', were introduced in the 1970s. (Museum collection)

The fifth headquarters was built at Chester on the site of an eleventh-century Benedictine nunnery; its construction involved the demolition of some nineteenth-century militia buildings. The new headquarters was opened by HRH the Duchess of Gloucester in July 1967. In 2003, the force moved to the present headquarters at Clemonds Hey, Winsford and this building was demolished to make way for a new civic building and hotel. (Cheshire Constabulary)

A young officer supervises the disinfecting of a farm visitor during the Foot and Mouth epidemic of 1967–8, during which many fine dairy herds were destroyed. The emergency lasted 224 days and both man-power and resources were fully stretched. In Cheshire, there were 1,021 outbreaks reported, with 150,000 animals having to be slaughtered at a cost of several million pounds, leaving a devastated farming community. (Cheshire Constabulary)

Cheshire Constabulary formed a shallow-water search unit in the late 1960s and it is pictured here displaying the equipment in use at that time. Later in the 1970s, a joint underwater search unit was formed from the Cheshire, North Wales, Merseyside and Greater Manchester forces. Today the North West Regional Underwater Search and Marine Unit is comprised of twelve officers drawn from all the north-west forces and North Wales. (Museum collection)

The panda scheme in Cheshire was initially introduced at Chester in 1967. The first vehicles purchased were Ford Anglia saloons seen here assembled on the castle forecourt. The following year the scheme was introduced countywide with the Vauxhall Viva being the vehicle of choice. The panda scheme revolutionised the traditional foot-beat system by placing more officers in cars and introduced the personal radio. (Museum collection)

Following the introduction of the panda scheme at Chester in 1967, it was adopted throughout the county in 1968. Here the new Vauxhall Viva saloons allocated to the Stockport Division are inspected by the mayor, accompanied by the Divisional Commander Chief Superintendent Tom Walker. The vehicles are lined up outside the Central Police Station at Lee Street. (Museum collection)

Vauxhall Viva panda cars assembled at Whitby Park Ellesmere Port in 1968 to launch the panda scheme in that area. The cars, headed by a motorcycle escort, paraded through the town, which is also the home of the car plant where the vehicles had been manufactured. (Museum collection)

Inspector Fred Hayhoe opens an advanced driving course at the driving school at Crewe in 1970. Looking on are the instructors, sergeants Arthur Williams and Ron Stockton. These courses lasted several weeks and were very intensive for the students in perfecting their driving skills and knowledge to the highest level of competence as an advanced police driver. The notice above the door serves to remind them of their responsibilities. (Museum collection)

The police launch *Charon* (pictured), which was mainly operational during the summer months of the 1960s and '70s to patrol the River Dee, in order to regulate the abundance of river traffic, enforce local bylaws and deal with any incidents occurring on the river. By the early 1980s, the launch had been taken out of use. (Museum collection)

Sergeant Ken Sloan, Stockport Division Training Officer, pictured with schoolchildren on a visit to Stockport Police Station in 1972. Constable Pat Barry is looking on. Schools' liaison to this day remains an important aspect of community involvement within the force. (Carmen Williams)

In 1970, the force were honoured to be visited by His Royal Highness the Duke of Edinburgh. He is seen here inspecting officers at Stockport Divisional Headquarters and is speaking with Constable Jack Taylor about his days in the Royal Navy as a gunner during the Second World War. Looking on are Chief Superintendent Geoffrey Pugh (far left) and Superintendent Bert Spencer. (Museum collection)

Detective Chief Superintendent Arthur Benfield explaining details of the Moors Murders case to His Royal Highness at Police Headquarters in a specially arranged display, which included photographs of Brady and Hindley and their victims. Arthur Benfield headed the investigation from Hyde Police Station in 1965, which also included officers from the Manchester and Lancashire forces. Benfield retired from the force in 1972. (Cheshire Constabulary)

Pictured here is His Royal Highness attending a briefing of officers at Chester, prior to them commencing patrol duties. He is accompanied by Chief Constable Henry Watson and Divisional Chief Superintendent Bob Talbot. (Museum collection)

His Royal Highness pictured on the esplanade at Police Headquarters, Chester, with senior officers and representatives of the Police Federation and Superintendents' Association during his visit to the force in 1970. Seated to his right is Mr Henry Watson, the chief constable, and to his left, Mr C.L.S. Cornwall-Legh, Chairman of the Police Authority. The Cheshire Constabulary at that time had a strength of over 3,000 officers. (Museum collection)

Runcorn constable, John Watson (on the left) liaising with an officer of the Manchester Ship Canal Police at Runcorn Docks in 1971. The Ship Canal Police had jurisdiction throughout the entire length of the canal, including the docks at Runcorn and a close relationship existed with local police. (Museum collection)

An officer of the Birkenhead Division seen here in 1971 talking with two foreign seamen at the Tranmere Oil Terminal. The Dock Estate Sub Division based at Tower Road Police Station was responsible for policing the Mersey Dock and Harbour Board Estate. (Museum collection)

'Hey Sarge, do you think she'll be secure enough from local thieves?' A Birkenhead sergeant and constable of the Docks Sub Division patrolling the graving dock in 1971. (Museum collection)

In 1971, an event recorded in the *Guinness Book of Records* was the movement by road of three sections of an oil cracking plant from Birkenhead to Ellesmere Port. At the time, it was the largest load ever moved by road and it took eight hours to complete the journey. The operation necessitated the temporary removal of traffic lights and other roadside furniture, and involved a large number of officers and resources. (Museum collection)

Members of the Special Constabulary being inspected at the Force Training Centre at Crewe (*c.* 1972) by Mr C.L.S. Cornwall-Legh, Chairman of the Police Authority. Special constables were first recruited during the First World War and played a vital role in both world wars. They remain very much an integral part of modern-day policing. (Museum collection)

A view of Tarporley Police Station in 1972 when a sergeant and small section of constables were based there. The station, built of sandstone and containing three cells, was opened in 1909 to replace an earlier station on the same site. It ceased to be a police station in the 1980s, and is now privately owned and is Grade II listed. (Museum collection)

In November 1979, two women were murdered at Boarded Barn Cottage, near Congleton. A major investigation was launched that resulted in the arrest of three men from Huddersfield, who were each sentenced to thirty years' imprisonment. Detective Superintendent Tom Brooks (forefront), who led the investigation, is pictured with the incident room staff at Congleton Police Station. Computers had yet to be introduced and records were indexed on a card system. (Mike Smyth)

A portrait of Chief Superintendent Arthur Morris taken around the time of his retirement in 1979, when he was in charge of the Macclesfield Division. The son of Superintendent Frederick Morris, he joined the force in 1939 and had a distinguished career both in uniform and as a detective. Morris was awarded the Queen's Police Medal in 1978. (Museum collection)

7

RECREATION

Members of the North Wirral Division football team pictured in 1896. The officer second from left sitting on the ground is Henry Sheasby, who joined the force in 1893 and who was later to become chief constable of the Macclesfield Borough Police. (Museum collection)

The Warrington Borough Police swimming team (*c.* 1920). The Barr brothers are seated in the centre row with John (far right) and Thomas (far left). Both were 6ft 4in in height and had left Clydebank in 1909 and 1910 respectively to join the Warrington force. Both enlisted in the Grenadier Guards during the First World War. Chief Constable Martin Nicholls is seated centre. (Museum collection)

Members of Chester City Police football team (*c.* 1927) boarding the team coach outside the police station in Princess Street at the side of the Town Hall. They are thought to be on their way to take part in an important match, possibly the league final. The team mascot can be seen perched on the windscreen. (Museum collection)

The Chester City Police football team pictured in 1927, believed to be the same team seen boarding the coach in the earlier photograph. Details of the team members and their footballing achievements are unknown. (Museum collection)

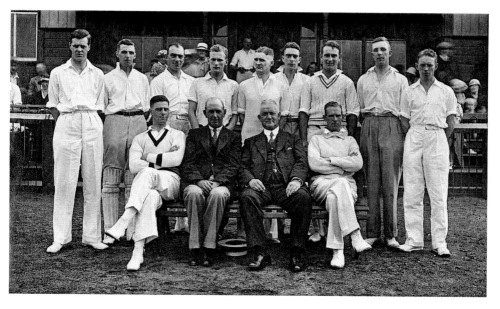

The Headquarters and Broxton Divisions cricket team, pictured in 1934, when they won the county championship against Crewe Division at the LMR ground at Rainbow Street, Crewe. The winners declared at 172 for 9 wickets with Crewe being all out for 125. Superintendent Morgan of Broxton Division is seated in the photograph (third from left). (Museum collection)

Captain Archibald Hordern AFC, pictured at the microphone, served as Cheshire's chief constable during 1934 and 1935. On joining the force, he established the Inter Divisional Athletics Sports Shield and can be seen here presenting it to Superintendent Morgan of the Broxton and Headquarters Division. Apart from the war years, the shield was presented annually until 1990. Captain Hordern left Cheshire to become the chief constable of Lancashire. (Museum collection)

Altrincham Division won the Grace Tug of War trophy in 1938. Frederick Morris, Divisional Superintendent, is seated centre. The team standing from left: constables Lomax, Pocock, Smith, Lamb, Batty, Thorogood, Lawrence and Cartlidge. (Museum collection)

Wirral Division cricket team, winners of the Chief Constables Cup in the 1948 season. Pictured standing from left: H. Jones (Umpire), constables Nutter, Williams, Blackwell, Hulmes, Beesley, Medley and MacIntosh. Seated from left: Sergeant Barker, Constable Snape, Superintendent Weatherby, Assistant Chief Constable Alexander Henderson, Superintendent Powell and constables Greenhalgh and Mackreth. (Museum collection)

Warrington Borough Police football team pictured in 1951. Standing from left: Constable Blunt, Sergeant Hyde, constables McLoughlin, Innes, Sedgebeer, Wells, Hawthorn, Lamerick, Sanders and Palin. Seated from left: constables Gordon, Arthur, Leech, Hanberry, Edwards and Pennington. The achievements of the team are unknown. (Museum collection)

Crewe Division cricket team (below) winners of the Chief Constables Cup 1951 season. Standing from left: umpire, Constable Clarke, Sergeant Fitton, Constable Astbury, Cadet Ankers, Constable Ikin, Cadet Horne, Detective Constable Hennell, Constables Goolding, Crossley, umpire. Seated from left: constables Scott and Healey, Superintendent O'Sullivan, Assistant Chief Constable Alexander Henderson, Superintendent J. Henderson and constables Goulding (Captain) and King. (Museum collection)

Crewe Division winners of the Grace Tug of War trophy in 1953. Standing from left: constables Middleton, Jones, Musker, Lowe, Farish and Bellingham. Seated: Constable Goolding, Superintendent J. Henderson, Sergeant Cooper and Constable Jacobs. (Museum collection)

In 1953, the Cheshire Constabulary swimming team won the National Police Life Saving Championships. The team and officials are pictured, standing from left: constables Palfreyman, Ratledge, Robotham, Heron and Sellwood. Seated from left: Constable McClellan, Detective Inspector Hanson, Assistant Chief Constable George Durnell, Inspector Murray and Constable Carter. The Cheshire force was renowned for its achievements in life saving competitions during the 1950s and '60s. (Museum collection)

North East Cheshire Division winners of the Chief Constables Cup, 1952/53 season. Standing from left: constables Banbury, Mackreth, Kirkham and Fairhall, Cadet Shaw, constables Humphreys, Merrick and Winning. Seated from left: constables Wood and Smith, Chief Inspector Welsh, Assistant Chief Constable George Durnell (Assistant Chief Constable), Superintendent Wilkes and constables Wilson and Barton. (Museum collection)

Runcorn Division winners of the Chief Constables Cup, 1953/54 season. Standing from left: Sergeant Hayes, constables Boney, Flood, Taylor, Argent, Arnold and Wilson. Seated from left: constables Howard and Morris, Cadet Hough, Chief Constable Banwell, Superintendent Wilkes, constables Finlayson, Coombes and Buckley. (Museum collection)

Macclesfield Division, winners of the Inter Divisional Bowls League, 1956 season. Standing from the left: Sergeant Cooper, constables Edwards, Davies and Roberts and Sergeant Bradley. Seated from left: Inspector Armstrong, Constable Mason, Superintendent Watson and Inspector Thompson. (Museum collection)

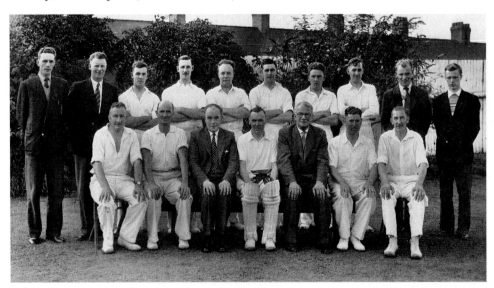

North East Cheshire Division cricket team winners of the Chief Constables Cup, 1958 season. Standing from left: constables Humphreys, Goulden, Bowers, Potts, Robinson, Blythin, Hughes, Ellis and Kershaw and Cadet Rothwell. Seated from left: Constable Bellingham, Chief Inspector Lewtas, Chief Superintendent O'Sullivan, Constable Mackreth, Chief Constable Banwell and constables Rees and Crabtree. (Museum collection)

Macclesfield Division winners of the Chief Constables Cup, 1956/57 season. Standing from left: constables Wilkins, Hughes, Humphreys, Prestwich, Mills and Jones. Seated from left: Detective Constable Suckley, constables Wood and Slater, Superintendent Watson, Chief Constable Banwell, constables Smith, Bailey and Wilkinson. (Museum collection)

North East Cheshire Division, runners up against Northwich Division in the Chief Constables Cup, 1957/58. Standing from left: constables Goulden, Bridges, Knight, -?-, Argent, Robinson, Davies and Detective Constable Harrison (Team Manager). Seated from left: Cadet Rothwell, Constable Leach, Chief Superintendent O'Sullivan, Constable White (captain), Chief Constable Banwell and constables Benbow and Bayley. (Museum collection)

Participating members of the Chester City and Headquarters Division pictured (*c.* 1960) after winning the Inter Divisional Athletics Sports Shield. The combined divisions won the shield in five successive years from 1957–61. Superintendent A. Elliott of the City Division and his Deputy Chief Inspector W. Lowe (seated centre) are supporting the shield. (Museum collection)

In 1962, the force won the No. 1 District Competition in the Police National Life Saving Championship. Standing from left: Constable Palfreyman, Sergeant Ratledge, Detective Constable Tushingham and constables Apperley and Nickson. Seated from left: Constable Burton, Superintendent Murray, Chief Constable Banwell, Inspector Coleman and Constable Rustage. (Museum collection)

The Cheshire Constabulary first-aid team pictured in 1963, after winning the Ambulance Challenge Shield. Teams from many of the north-west forces competed annually for this coveted award. Standing from left: constables Alan Spann, Geoffrey Broomhall, Ken Lancaster and Lew Bleasdale. Seated: Sergeant Jack Dyas and Chief Constable Henry Watson. (Museum collection)

Cheshire Policewomen's first-aid team pictured after winning the National Policewomen's First-Aid Championships at Porchester Hall, London in February 1964. Top, from left: constables Lambert (Altrincham) and Hilton (Northwich). Below, from left, Detective Constable Young (Wirral), Inspector Attwater (Captain) and Constable Owen (Macclesfield). (Museum collection)

Macclesfield Division first-aid team pictured in April 1968, after winning the Opher Shield in the competition held at Barrow in Furness. Standing from the left: constables Gordon Swindells, Leslie Bugh, Colin Perks and Fred Johnson. Seated: Constable Ray Davies, Chief Superintendent Percy Wilkes and Sergeant Jack Burton. (Museum collection)

Members of the Special Constabulary Stockport Division pictured in 1970 receiving an award. Seated from left: Chief Superintendent Geoffrey Pugh, Divisional Commander, Assistant Chief Constable McIntosh, Special Chief Inspector Walmsley, holding the cup, Chief Superintendent Joan Hunt and Chief Inspector Roy Cross. Standing far left: Sergeant Ken Sloan, Divisional Training Officer. (Carmen Williams)

If you enjoyed this book, you may also be interested in ...

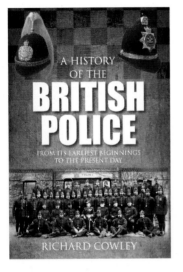

A History of the British Police: From its Earliest Beginnings to the Present Day
RICHARD COWLEY

Having expelled the Norse invaders from his kingdom, Alfred the Great wanted to ensure that it remained peaceful and law-abiding. He therefore appointed a shire reeve for each county, who was responsible for maintaining the King's Peace. As the population grew, magistrates and parish constables would become the main weapons in the fight against crime, and, as the Industrial Revolution changed the nature of society, the organised constabularies that we know today began to evolve, most notably with Robert Peel's establishment of the Metropolitan Police. This book is a comprehensive account of the British police force and makes interesting reading for anyone interested in the history of policing in Britain.

978 0 7524 5891 5

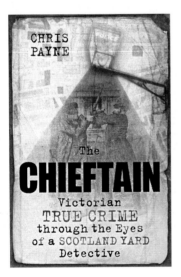

The Chieftain: Victorian True Crime Through the Eyes of a Scotland Yard Detective
CHRIS PAYNE

George Clarke joined the Metropolitan Police in 1841. Though a 'slow starter', his career took off when he was transferred to the small team of detectives at Scotland Yard in 1862, where he became known as 'The Chieftain'. This book paints the most detailed picture yet published of detective work in mid-Victorian Britain, covering 'murders most foul', slums and 'Society', the emergence of terrorism related to Ireland, and Victorian frauds. In this fascinating book, the author (Clarke's great-great-grandson) has researched his subject in depth and has captured the essence of Victorian crime and detection, using widespread sources of information, including many of Clarke's own case reports.

978 0 7524 5667 6

Visit our website and discover thousands of
other History Press books.

www.thehistorypress.co.uk